Journey
P O E M S

WADE HUDSON

Third World Press Foundation
Chicago

Third World Press Foundation
Publishers since 1967
Chicago

First Edition
Printed in the United States of America

ISBN: 978-0-88378-417-4
22 21 20   6 5 4 3 2 1

DEDICATION

This book is dedicated to
my mother, Lurline Jones Hudson
my father, Wade Hudson, Sr.
those from my hometown, Mansfield, Louisiana
and other Black folks who dared to be.

CONTENTS

FAMILY

PERSONAL REFLECTION

AUTHOR'S NOTE

While growing up in Mansfield, Louisiana during the 1950s and 1960s, I would sit on my front porch with a pad and pen, sometimes a pencil, in hand. As other youngsters played their games, running and enjoying the hot summer weather and accommodating winters, I wrote poetry. I was around eight years old when I started writing.

Writing poems was my outlet. It was my way to connect to other ways of thinking. It was how I expressed the thoughts and ideas I felt were different from the ideas and thoughts of those around me. What was the world like beyond my small hometown cocoon? Were White people different? What about Black people? What would it feel like to walk the streets of Harlem and catch a James Brown show at the famed Apollo Theater? What was Tuskegee Institute like, the Black college I had read about in a Booker T. Washington biography? Students excelled there and it was where the famous Tuskegee Airmen trained.

In school, I enjoyed reading poetry, at least, the poetry that was in our school textbooks. Robert Frost's "Stopping by the Woods on a Snowy Evening" and "The Road Less Traveled," Walt Whitman's "Oh Captain, My Captain," William Ernest Henley's "Invictus," and almost any poem by Edna St. Vincent Millay, were among the first poems to resonate with me. I still can recite Henley's "Invictus" from memory!

When I arrived at Southern University, a historically Black university located in Baton Rouge, Louisiana, after graduating from all-Black Desoto High School, my world changed in so many ways. It was there that I was introduced to the works of Black poets, novelists, thinkers, and academicians. Inspired by this newly found treasury of Black literary accomplishments, I began to write poems at a brisker pace. The work produced by these Black writers spoke directly to me. Many of Langston Hughes's poems were about people I knew and situations to which I could relate. Paul Laurence Dunbar's poems captured the lives of people that I knew when I was growing up. The Black kid in Richard Wright's coming of age memoir *Black Boy* was like me in so many respects. Zora Neale Hurston, W.E.B. DuBois, Countee Cullen, Gwendolyn Brooks, Claude McKay, Margaret Walker, Sterling A. Brown—discovering these literary greats and others validated my efforts to write about my world and infused me with a greater sense of purpose. Through their works, I understood that writing was more than simply a literary pursuit. It was also a platform to fight for change. The Nigerian writer Chinua Achebe expressed it best, "The writer cannot expect to be excused from the task of reeducation and regeneration that must be done. In fact, he should march right in front."

At Southern, there were opportunities to read my work at gatherings with other writers, where musicians often provided live background music. Some of my poems were published in *Southern Digest*, the university's student newspaper. During this time poets and writers of the Black Arts Movement caught my attention. Haki Madhubuti's *Think Black* impacted me profoundly because the poems in his slim collection helped me to focus more clearly on the importance of knowing who I was and the necessity of a Black identity and Black aesthetic.

Although I loved writing poetry, I also enjoyed writing plays. While in high school, I wrote and directed a play that was performed by fellow students. I joined my high school drama group and acted in several student productions. At Southern, I wrote a play that was covered in the daily newspaper when it was produced. Playwriting, then, replaced poetry as my literary love. Occasionally, an idea would emerge that I had to express through poetry, but playwriting was my primary focus.

More than three decades ago, my wife Cheryl and I founded Just Us Books, Inc, a children's book publishing company. Since then, most of my time has been spent building a successful company to address the need for books for children and young adults that present Black experiences, Black characters, and that focus on Black history and culture.

After penning a poem for a 2018 anthology, *We Rise, We Resist, We Raise Our Voices,* which Cheryl and I edited, my desire to write poetry returned. Over several months, I wrote dozens of poems. The process seemed to flow seamlessly as it did during those earlier years. I decided I wanted to publish a poetry collection and even added a few poems I'd written in the 1970s. These poems address subjects such as love, family, Black folks, Black culture and history and personal reflection.

Like Langston Hughes, Gwendolyn Brooks, Mari Evans and Haki Madhubuti before him, that little boy who sat on the steps of his home in Mansfield, Louisiana, writing poems about his world, now has a collection to share. The journey has come full circle. I am honored to share with you, *Journey, Poems.*

Journey
P O E M S

.

HOMETOWN

THOSE EARLY YEARS

It was a time of ease.
Of walking barefoot on dusty roads and paved but cracking streets.
High fiving neighbors and never missing a beat.
Berry picking and plum gathering for summertime fun,
Running shirtless in the blistering, hot summer sun.
Listening to the guitars everyone seemed to play.
Hearing stories about what it was like back in the day.

But it was a time to pause.
When wintertime came and things got tough.
Going hungry sometimes when meals weren't enough.
Kneeling at mother's bedside when she often got ill.
Praying that God and the doctor would quickly heal.
Watching TV commercials, admiring the products shown with a fuss.
Wishing the white kids who had them would one day be us.

It was a time of ease.
Vida Blue's fast ball whizzing past like you couldn't see.
Nestling in the glove of the catcher, my brother PG.
Cleontis's big glove, his father's gift to help him grow.
Greeting Ray Bogan's laser, bunny-hopped, baseball throw.
We all hit the field running, no time to lose.
When playing the game we loved can't fall victim to the blues.

But it was a time to pause.
The theater balcony where we were forced to go.
While white folks sat in the choice seats below.
Clothes had better fit, couldn't try them on.
They were all yours when you took them home.
A near deadly, meal, that old Jim Crow.
Fighting to spit it out, while trying to grow.

It was a time of ease.
All day Sunday gathering, worship-time at the country church.
Singing songs, giving thanks, couldn't praise Him too much!
Segregated school, taught Mary McLeod Bethune's way

5

Set the right course for a brand-new day.
Feeling the love like air, all around
To nurture, to sustain, to offer fertile ground.

But it was a time to pause.
Emmett Till's brutalized body frightened us in *Jet*.
Cops sent dogs to attack Black children, no hint of regret.
Black bodies lost to white hatred and contempt
If you were Black, no one's exempt.
Struggling to survive, determined to sustain.
Holding on to dignity's dying refrain.

It was a time of ease, a time to pause.
Side by side, both with cause.
Indelible marks they imprint to endure.
Modifying the reach of freedom's allure
A time of ease, a time to pause.
Side by side, both with cause.

THE OLD FOLKS

Those old men and women of my youth are gone.
Having held on for oh, so long.
Those old souls with bodies bent.
Too soon gray hair and hard time spent.
Nursing corns and callouses their work grew.
Aching bodies that rest could not renew.

Cotton fields and logging consumed their time.
Domestic work stretched their lives to a grind.
Yet they found enough light to illuminate the dark.
Enough joy to sometimes suspend misery so stark.
Faith enough to cast hope for a better tomorrow.
Ways to balance both joy and sorrow.
Yes, they are gone now. They are all gone.
But sometimes I feel their presence when I'm alone.
And I am encouraged! Encouraged by their grace.
That helps me find my own safe place!

GUITARS

Those guitar pickers from old Mansfield.
Could make guitars talk like BB's Lucille.
Bent those notes and stretched those strings.
Made those guitars do all sorts of things.

Must have been in the water is how they passed it down.
Bluesmen grew all over the town.
Played those guitars! Made those strings cry!
When the guitars talked no one asked why!

Got lost in the melody, the rhythm and the beat!
Played from memory. Didn't need music sheets.
Battered and bruised, many battle scars.
To escape for a while, they played their guitars.

MANCHILD IN THE PROMISED LAND

We sold cold drink bottles.
Two cents each they use to be.
Not worth much now, I'm told.
We carried them in bags, in little red wagons, in our arms.
We mowed lawns, too,
Sometimes barely making enough money
To meet the monthly note and pay for gas.

Independent, energetic kids we were.
Singing songs of the future,
Reciting creeds of survival.

We ran errands, too,
10 cents. 15 cents. 20 cents,
Depending on the type of job.
We cleaned yards of leaves
And dead grass.
Grown kids.
Facing life ahead of time.

Independent, energetic kids we were.
Singing songs of the future,
Reciting creeds of survival.

We grew up quickly.
Running. Screaming.
Crying. Laughing. Loving.
Unsure what it was all about.
Man child. Woman child.
Echoing voices from our ancestors
Spurring us onward.

Independent, energetic kids we were.
Singing songs of the future,
Reciting creeds of survival.

As years passed, realization settled in.
And like waking up from a dream the morning after,
We understood. Or did we
Really?
So, we ran through
Watts, Harlem, Newark and Detroit,
To relax for a while,
And to smile!

ELIZABETH NUMBER THREE
BAPTIST CHURCH

Hot Friday night on the mourner's seat.
Reverend Collins preaching, never missing a beat.
Felt the Holy Ghost stirring deep in my soul.
Something quite new about to unfold.
"When the change comes you'll really, really know."
That's what the elders said, and then I knew it was so.

Gave my hand to the pastor that sweltering night.
Gave my heart to God, and knew it was right.
Got baptized that Sunday, went down deep.
Came up anew, with promises to keep.
To let Jesus lead me, He knows the way.
Glad I let Him in that blessed day.

I met God at Elizabeth Number Three.
Where praise reigned down, unbridled and free.
Hearing, *"Thank you, Father, for all that you've done.*
Wouldn't take nothnin' for the race I've run."
Toils and snares faced day by day.
Elizabeth Number Three showed me the right way.

THE OLD PINE TREE

The corner of Mary and Gibbs was its perch.
On that corner it did command.
When passing it, didn't think too much.
Unless its cover was in your plan.

Tall but bending from decades of growth.
Enveloping the ground with needles and cones.
A Mary Street landmark of serious note.
A true community cornerstone.

The city-wide bus made its stop there.
Those who walked sought its cover from the sun.
Little children played silly games there.
It was where workers took a break when their day was done.

Those who drank more than their share
stopped to take a snooze every now and then.
Birds nested their baby chicks with care.
Seeking protection again and again.

Whatever happened to that tree?
Does it still command its place?
Giving shelter to all for free.
Or has it been cut down, leaving no trace?

MANSFIELD AT TEN

Sitting on the front porch,
Writing poems, short stories and songs.
Words pouring out like water from a faucet.
Where do they all come from?

Ten-year-old musings.
Ten-year-old thoughts — write them down!
Rocking the boat with words.
Pencil in hand and paper bound.

Mansfield days, Southern ways.
Must make sense of what I see.
Things seem always out of place.
Is this the way they ought to be?

"Yes sir, no sir," tip the hats.
Heads so bowed they might drop.
Moving to the side as whites pass by.
Me, praying it would all stop.

Ten-year-old musings,
Ten-year-old thoughts — write them down!
Recreate the reality.
Share the newness you have found.

A lonely craft writing is, they say.
It seems to be true.
For this ten-year-old son
With words bursting through.

Got to write them all down.
Before, like wandering smoke, they float.
It's a ten-year old's sensibilities.
And words that rock the boat.

HEROES, SHEROES
& FRIENDS

FOR AMIRI

I sought him.
Needing to hear his words of encouragement and support.
Needing to hear him say, *"Right on, my brother."*
I sought him.

Laboring with the pen, yearning to burst forth with purpose,
I tried to capture my own reality and the hope of,
A new tomorrow for my people.
But was the road right?

I sought him.
Small town cocoon, but giving birth to thoughts that examined,
analyzed, criticized and yes, condemned. Lonely. So lonely.
Alone with my thoughts.
I sought him.

From where did this yearning come?
This burning desire to create with pen?
What gave birth to those thoughts, those out-of-place thoughts?
Inside the small-town cocoon.

I sought him.
Nourished by *Preface to a Twenty Volume Suicide Note, The Dead
Lecturer* and *Blues People*. Inspired by *Dutchman and The Slave*.
Cocoon now burst open,
I sought him.

Connections are essential.
Rightful bearings are crucial.
A blessing from a distant traveler who has gleaned the way is a
grace.
We must push on to find our perch.

So, I sought him.
At Spirit House. Newark, NJ. 1967. Folders full of my thoughts.
He read them all and smiled afterwards, like a mentor to a mentee.
Then he said, *"Right on, young brother!"*
Yes, I sought the sage — and found him!

THE BARD OF CABRINI GREEN

Never held back, that Curtis Mayfield.
Knew what the truth would ultimately yield.
Love for his people so strong and sincere.
Poured from his lyrics, passionately and clear.

A Cabrini Green child. Northside. Chicago.
Heard about the lash and whip, faced Northern Jim Crow.
Knew music could be more than just hustle and flow.
So, he stepped up to write and sing, and became our hero.

People get ready, there's a train a coming.
All you need is faith to hear the diesel humming.
So, keep on pushin', you can't stop now.
Move up a little higher, some way, somehow.

"Cause we the people who are Darker than Blue.
Can't stand around this town, let what others say come true.
See, we're a winner, and everybody knows it too.
Got to keep on pushin', like our leaders tell us to.

Flowing from the pen of our own troubadour.
Songs recorded like none before.
Imploring us all to remove the yoke.
Encouraging. Chastising. And offering hope.

Keep on pushin' sang Martin Luther King.
All God's children *let freedom ring*.
Marching to the beat while protesting along.
Inspired by the words of a Mayfield song.

We'll never forget the role that he played.
We'll always remember the contributions he made.
We'll sing his songs. We'll *keep on pushin'* still.
And raise the name of Curtis Mayfield.

THE TRANE

Saxophonic melodies
Serenade my thoughts while
The light touch of her hand
Drapes my being with joy.
It is moments like these
That tempt one
To forget a dying environment,
A world on the avalanche of time.

Smooth sounds curl in
And out
Of me.
Lifting me. Upward, spiraling,
Nestling on soft, velvety
I got 'cha music vibrations —
Taking me by the hand and leading me
Into a state of peace and joy.

Blow
    Saxophonist.
        The essence
            Of you.
                The essence
                    Of me.
                        Show me
                            The essence
                              And blow
                                  My mind.
                              Sooth me.
                                    Crush them
                                      With your
                                        Music of truth.

A Love Supreme.
    A Love Supreme.
I want to reach out and grab those
Sounds. Caress them. Kiss them.
They are so true. So real. So honest.
Me and them. In a crescendo.
Blow my mind! Blow my mind!
My bones are your bass.
My heart is your drum.
And the honest tickling of my mind
Is your piano.
Take me where you are at.
Truth I want!
Love I want!
A Love Supreme.
    A Love Supreme.
Take me where you are at!
I don't want to miss the *"Trane."*

PIONEERS OF ROCK AND ROLL

Those 1940s musicians with their instruments in tow.
Started a kind of music never heard before.
With jazz, blues, and swing and a whole lot of soul.
They were the real pioneers of the music called Rock and Roll.

Everyone has heard about Elvis, Haley, and Freed.
History books brim with their so-called deeds.
But the 1940s musicians, those Black women and men,
have been robbed of their legacy again and again.

Louis Jordan and his Tympany Five
Got it all started, playing party music and rapping jive.
They topped the charts, both Black music and Pop.
When dancing to Louis's music no one wanted to stop!

Sister Rosetta Tharpe on the electric guitar.
From the very beginning this sister was a star.
From Gospel to R&B, she pioneered a style
that rock guitarists incorporated in their music profile.

Amos Milburn, Ivory Joe Hunter, just to name a few.
And all the others who never got their due.
Like The Fat Man—Antoine Domino
Wynonie Harris and his rocking combo.

So, when the story of Rock and Roll is told,
Don't leave the Black pioneers out of the fold.
They laid the foundation and sailed the ship.
Include their stories! — Don't flip the script!

FOR YOU, VERA MITCHELL

She came on the scene like a shooting star.
Announced herself like an avatar.
Firing on all cylinders, an engine at peak.
Breathing fresh air and plugging every leak.
With Vera Mitchell, very little got by.
Couldn't shoot her down, so you just didn't try.

Holding court in kitchens, sometimes in living rooms.
Blasting out her intellect, while others folded too soon.
Young and brash and so self-assured.
Shouting out indignities, our folks had endured.
Never missing a beat, grasping all the sounds.
Rap on Vera, run it all down.

A Chicago lady. A Chicago Mom.
Moved to Champaign to sing her song.
Some say shooting stars all fade one day.
But Vera's special star just shone another way.
Mothering college students, sharing wisdom with care.
Still blasting out her intellect to those who would dare.

So, my dear Vera, you did write your book.
You gave your love with all it took.
Our sacred ancestors now hold your hand.
All applaud and salute, the race you ran.
So, blast your intellect with a style supreme.
Surely Zora, Langston, and Bethune know what it all means.

YOUNG MICHAEL BROWN

Young Michael Brown was gunned down today.
Yet another brother got in the way.
Old racial animus still holding sway.
As in the past will there be no debt to pay?

Young Michael Brown is not here anymore.
Another family's son added to the score.
Black lives stuffed out, thieves pounding at the door.
Spitting out bullets, guns screaming for more.

Young Michael! Young Michael! I cry for you, son.
For Trayvon, Jordan, Eric, all the others gone.
Life so dear — gone — in a flash.
How long ago was the whip and the lash?

Been in the struggle all my days.
Victories and defeats, every step of the way.
Faith and hope continued to stay.
Both were tested when Michael was killed today.

But the struggle continues, no time to suspend.
Stand up! Speak Out! Implore all to join in!
Ida B, Freddie D, Harriet and Martin, all send
This powerful message, the quest for freedom never ends.

THOSE GREAT BLACK WOMEN
THEY KEEP ON COMING!
In Honor of Sterling A. Brown

Phyllis Wheatley. Harriet Tubman.
Sojourner Truth. Ellen Craft.
Biddy Mason. Mary Patterson.
Frances Ellen Harper. Edmonia Lewis.
They keep coming!

Susan King Taylor. Fannie Coppin.
Charlotte Ray. Mary Mahoney.
Ida B. Wells. Mary Church Terrell.
Madame C.J. Walker. Maggie Lena Walker.
They keep coming!

Amy Jacques Garvey. Lucy Laney.
Mary McLeod Bethune. Nannie Burroughs.
Bessie Coleman. Josephine Baker.
Bessie Smith. Marian Anderson.
They keep coming!

Meta Warrick Fuller. Zora Neale Hurston.
Augusta Savage. Lois Mallou Jones.
Georgia Johnson. Margaret Walker.
Gwendolyn Brooks. Marian Anderson.
They keep coming!

Katherine Dunham. Alice Coachman.
Willye White. Juanita Hall.
Frankie Muse Freeman. Autherine Lucy.
Althea Gibson. Wilma Rudolph.
They keep coming!

Joanne Robinson. Rosa Parks.
Lorraine Hansberry. Daisey Bates.
Ella Baker. Fannie Lou Hamer.
Dorothy Height. Coretta Scott King.
They keep coming!

Diane Nash. Angela Davis.
Shirley Chisholm. Barbara Jordan.
Maya Angelou. Patricia Harris.
Coretta Scott King. Constance Baker Motley.
They keep coming!

Kathleen Cleaver. Elaine Brown.
Nikki Giovanni. Sonia Sanchez.
Nina Simone. Toni Morrison.
Shirley Chisholm. Audra Lorde.
They keep coming!

Mae Jemison. Aretha Franklin.
Toni Cade Bambara. Jane C. Wright.
Alice Walker. Toni Morrison.
Oprah Winfrey. Marian Wright Edelman.
They keep coming!

Aretha Franklin. Vashti McKenzie.
Cathy Hughes. Maxine Waters.
Serena Williams. Michelle Obama.
Jacqueline Woodson. Patrisse Cullors.
They keep coming! They keep coming!
On and on and on!
They just keep on coming!

UNSUNG HEROES

Their names
are
not
known.

Their deeds
are
forever
lost.

The price
they
paid
unrecognized.

But willingly
they
accepted
the cost.

They stood
to
advance
the cause.

They fought
for
higher
ground,

In cities
in
towns
and in villages.

Their relentlessness
knew
no
bounds.

Where would
we
be
without them?

Though we
know
not
who they are.

It's King
and Douglass.
Tubman and
Sojourner Truth.

Their contributions
are lifted
higher
by far.

But the quest
for freedom
would be
stymied.

If not
for
those
unsung.

No.
We know
not
their names.

But relish
the work
of freedom
they have done.

FOR THE LOST LIVES

If we could bring back
those lives departed
who didn't quite live yet.
If only we could show our loss
And sorrow with an *"I'm sorry,"* or a *"forgive me."*
Perhaps they would understand.
Perhaps they would understand
And pity us.
But in this season
We find many reasons.

Perhaps they would understand.
Understand why so many just stand by.
But there once was a time when
When we loved life.
And lived happily and peacefully.
And smiled. And laughed. Gutsy laughs.
Laughs that would damage the ear drum.
If only we could bring back those days,
So they wouldn't have to understand.
But in this season
We find many reasons.

But summer must — and —
Will come soon.
If only we could throw away
the winter things.
If only we could rid ourselves
Of the winter coldness.
If only we could all hold our children.
Love our children to life.
But in this season
We find many reasons.

VOICES OF ANGELS

Lift every voice and sing!
Aretha did.
Billie and Bessie did
it for years.
Reaching deep.
Pulling out/throwing-at-you
sounds that astound.
       Arethas
            Billies
      Bessies
Saw one yesterday. In church.
Sings for pleasure, though/for the Lord.
But she reached me
Like Aretha did.
Sent me sprawling into
An ocean of down-home soul.
A bed of blackness.
She comes from the church.
And can get notes nobody
Can write down.
Look around.
See the angels.
One in the church near you.
Maybe two.
The singing angels.

THE STRUGGLE

THE FREEDOM BRIGADE

Through the annals of history they kept marching.
From slave ship beginnings their plans were made
To remove the yoke that enslaved them.
They were the mighty freedom brigade.

> The lot was not their making.
> The destiny they did not choose.
> Who would want to be property?
> Brutalized and abused?
> But shackles could not contain them.
> The whip could not dissuade.
> Even death could not forfeit
> the oath of freedom they made.
> Decades came and decades went.
> Sometimes the struggle seemed lost.
> But Frederick Douglass cried out.
> Nat Turner paid the ultimate cost.
> Onward they did continue,
> Harriet Tubman leading the way.
> Reaching for the higher ground
> Jubilee on the way.

Through the annals of history they kept marching.
From slave ship beginnings their plans were made
To remove the yoke that enslaved them.
They were the mighty freedom brigade.

> Time to shout *Hallelujah!*
> Slavery has been slain.
> But only for a little while
> Jim Crow is slavery back again.
> Can't afford to rest.
> Never made it up the hill.
> For the mighty freedom fighters,
> Frontline beckons still.
> Keep marching and protesting,
> Singing "Freedom over Me."

Picket signs and boycott lines.
Don't you wanna be free?
It's the ballot or the bullet!
Was Brother Malcolm's decree.
Try it all, my people.
Try it all to be free.

Through the annals of history they kept marching.
From slave ship beginnings their plans were made
To remove the yoke that enslaved them.
They were the mighty freedom brigade.

Some names are legendary.
Others a blink in the night.
All made courageous stands,
As they joined the perilous fight.
They charged on toward freedom.
They held their banner high.
Pressed on to break the chains
That would shackle you and I.
No, the struggle is not over.
Still more battles to be won.
But what would be our state,
If they had not marched on?
Giving all they had.
To contest freedom's foes.
Let's never ever forget them.
They are our heroes.

Through the annals of history they kept marching.
From slave ship beginnings their plans were made
To remove the yoke that enslaved them.
They were the mighty freedom brigade.

SOUL OF AMERICA

From the Motherland of Africa, on ships bound for the Atlantic.
Chained together in hulls, desperate cries shrilled and frantic.
Countless claimed by the ocean water, African burial ground so far away.
Those that made it vowed to remember the land they left that faithful day.

Destined for the auction block, names strategically removed.
Sold to the highest bidder, the rebellious quickly subdued.
A free labor force soon created to make America great.
Enslaved laborers forced to endure America's greed and hate.

Listen to the hopeful music, the melodies so heartfelt and strong.
See the rhythm of the dances, the prayers that last all night long.
They signal a rooted courage, a determined will to survive.
Folks laying an enduring foundation, to keep their people alive.

It started from the very beginning. American forefathers said, "No!"
You cannot be a part of us. You're just a lowly Negro!
So our Ancestors built institutions to provide for their own
And established a Black America, a place to belong.

So many inventions and battles fought and won.
Despite the many setbacks, the march kept moving on.
Explain it! Explain it! What was at the core?
Making something out of nothing and adding even more!

Nearly four hundred years have gone, and tall we now stand.
But facing new challenges that threaten our Ancestor's plan,
Of a brand new reality, for their daughters and their sons.
Dare not lose the legacy, and hard-fought victories won.

PEOPLE OF THE BOAT

See them
    In Cuba
    In Jamaica
    In Brazil
    In Panama
    In Trinidad
    In the USA
People of the Boat.

Catch their style
    In food
    In music
    In dance
    In art
    In dress
    In talk
People of the Boat.

Witness their will
    To survive
    To overcome
    To achieve
    To struggle
    To live
    To be free
People of the Boat.

From Africa home
    Over sea
    Over land
    In shackles
    To be sold
    Economic foundation
    Cultural heart and soul
People of the Boat.

Watch them fly
> To create
> To invent
> To explore
> To discover
> To climb
> To surpass

We are people of the Boat.
People of the Boat.
PEOPLE OF THE BOAT!

ON BEING A NEGRO

Suspicious silence.
Don't know whether to run
or stand.
It be's that way sometimes.
Caught in a state of terror.
Heart throbbing.
Eyes popping,
out of the head!
Don't know whether to run
or stand.

Mind dripping,
sweat pouring
down the Black face.
Scared to death!
Whirling, spinning.
What to do?
Don't know whether to run
or stand!

A CLARION CALL

I would give my life if I could,
To bring more sanity and increase the good.
Would give my right arm, my left leg, too.
To decrease the pain our young are going through.

Where are the elders, the prophets and the sages?
Are they all lost to by-gone ages?
We need them now more than ever before.
To bind up the wounds and stop the blood flow.

Where are the fathers, the princes and the kings?
Standing watch at the gate, defenders of the Dream.
Where are the mothers, the princesses and queens?
Holding firm to the family circle and all that it means?

Who opened the gate, to let in despair?
And let cancerous cells infiltrate the air?
Under siege now, *All hands-on deck!*
Need everyone, to stop this wreck.

Blood on the streets. Blood in the halls.
Children killing children. It's a clarion call.
We have answered the call many times before.
Need to muscle up again, and answer once more.

WHAT SHALL WE TELL YOU?

What shall we tell you when our world sometimes seems dark and uninviting?

What shall we tell you when hateful words that wound and bully are thrown like bricks against a wall, shattering into debris?

What shall we tell you when respect for others and treating others as we wish to be treated appear as yesterday's borrowed wish?

What shall we tell you when our differences are juggled like fragile eggs that could be smashed at a moment's impulse?

What shall we tell you? What shall we tell you?

We shall tell you that love like cream in milk will rise to the top and hatred and distrust will be revealed as imposters.

We shall tell you that peace desirable as a restful night after a long day at play is not far away. Reach for it.

We shall tell you that respect for others, like a delicious ice cream bar dripping on holding fingers tastes better than contempt.

We shall tell you that we love you, all of you! And because we love you, we will be there to help bring light to dark places.

We will be there with peace and justice as our weapons and love as a soothing salve to comfort and embrace.

We shall tell you that because we will be there for you, always be there for you, it will be all right! It will be all right!

First published in *We Rise, We Resist, We Raise Our Voices,* copyright 2018, edited by Wade Hudson and Cheryl Hudson, published by Crown Books for Young Readers.

MESSAGE TO OUR YOUNG

There is hope.
No need to despair.
Take up your cause,
With determination and care.
Others have gone before.
Look what they have done.
No, it wasn't easy.
No race is easy to run.
Harriet Tubman's tenacity.
Frederick Douglass' flair.
Martin King's powerful words.
Barack Obama's dare.
Carried the baton of freedom —
Helped the freedom train to run.
You can help power the engine, too.
Your turn has just begun.

MUCH NEEDED CONVERSATION

You say you are tired of it.
You say it's time to let it go.
You say it's different now.
Those old days are no more.

Slavery was bad, you say.
But a hundred plus years have passed.
Yes, Jim Crow was awful.
But his terror just couldn't last.

You cringe when you hear them, you say,
Those talks about long ago.
Of marches, protests, and lynchings.
It's time to let them go.

It's a brand-new day, you say.
The world is different at last.
We've overcome much of it.
Time to let go of the past.

We should not frown, you say.
Our past should not be a trope.
We should move on, you say.
Not hold on to it like a rope.

But listen to me clearly,
My dear youthful friend.
Remember this rallying cry.
The quest for freedom never ends.

The challenges may be camouflaged.
They may dress up to deceive.
But you will be snatched up quickly.
When you unwittingly believe.

You must be ever vigilant.
Hold on to the ancestors' call.
Theirs was a continuous struggle.
That could not bear a stall.

Yes, there have been victories.
And those we ought to claim.
But the race is not finished.
More distance still remains.

The past is prologue to the future.
Both coalesce in history's sweep.
So, don't dismiss your people's journey.
Add your leg to help make it complete.

IT'S YOUR TIME

Kick it!
Kick it!
Kick it to the curb.
It's your time now.
So, kick it!
Kick it!
Kick it to the curb!

You've been bound too long.
You've been shaded too often.
You've been checked too much.
You've been passed over too many times.

So, kick it!
Kick it!
Kick it to the curb!

You've been made to wait.
You've been pushed to the side.
You've had to hold back.
You've had to mute your song.

So, Kick it!
Kick it!
Kick it to the curb!

Time to write your own story.
Time to sing your own tune.
Time to weave your own tapestry.
Time to create your own world.

You can do it!
If you kick it!
Kick it!
Kick it to the curb!

All that's in your way.
Kick it!
All that's there to muzzle you.
Kick it!
The *don'ts*.
Kick them!
The *Can'ts*.
Kick them!
The *What ifs*.
Kick them!
No time to hold back.
Just kick it!
Kick it!
Kick it all to the curb!
It's your time now.
You can do it!
If you kick it to the curb!

FAMILY

REMEMBERING MY FATHER
Wade Hudson, Sr. (1919-2015)

Old Jim Crow is a heinous creature,
a many-headed monster with frightening features.
A segregation-colored, distorted face.
Exacting its evil because of race.
My father knew old Jim very well.
Endured his reign for a long, long spell.
Went to Europe to fight for peace.
But Jim Crow's terror still didn't cease.
He played his role to help win the war.
All the while questioning, *"What was it for?"*

He came back home and settled down.
Old Jim Crow still hanging around.
He had dreams, there is no dispute.
But were they all just rendered moot?
Did they dry up like Langston's raisin in the sun?
As he chose a very different race to run.
He taught the games that we all played,
dissecting the plans that we all made.
Fathering business was at his core.
Deep within, still wanting more.

People die, but what about dreams?
Do they dissipate when there is no steam?
Or can they, like a baton, be passed on,
to allow others to make the run?
I declare it is a continuous race,
that connects us all in this broadening place.
Rest on, Father, in that distant sleep.
We hold the dreams you wanted to keep.

REMEMBERING MY MOTHER
Lurline Jones Hudson (1923-2018)

She was not the CEO of a Fortune 500 company.
She was not a doctor who discovered the cure for a menacing disease.
She did not lead a movement that knocked down doors of discrimination and racism.
She didn't write award-winning books or record popular songs.
She was considered a simple woman, born and raised in a Southern town with its Southern ways and segregation caste.

Perhaps, locked up inside her, never to be explored,
was the potential to have been
a pioneering doctor, a history-changing lawyer or the head of her own restaurant chain.
Yet her life was so much more meaningful than what Jim Crow sought to render.
She mastered the roles that she could embrace.
No woman could have been a more caring, loving and supportive mother.
Her guiding hands and curated wisdom nurtured the village.

Her heart and arms were open to all. There were no strangers to her.
Her faith could move mountains, and often did.
Troubled ones sought her for they knew she would care.
Her legacy is replete with helping hands given, encouragements offered and lives impacted in the most profound ways.
"I love you!" was the soundtrack of her connection with those whom she touched.

She was not the head of a big corporation.
Nor was she responsible for a great invention noted by historians.
She wasn't the first to reach a great achievement.
She was considered a simple woman.
Yet she touched lives in extraordinary ways and that lifted her
To unforgettable status!

MY FAMILY

I come from a big family.
A big, Black family.
A loud talking, foot stomping family.
A family of dreamers and planners and searchers and reachers.
Yeah, I come from a big family.

I come from a big family.
A family of boys to men,
Girls to women.
Year by year, behind each other like steps on a ladder.
Yeah, I come from a big family.

I come from a big family.
A family of lovers and loved.
A clutching family.
A hang in there, get it done, back slapping clad.
Yeah, I come from a big family.

I come from a big family.
Down South in your bones family.
Finger-licking, mac & cheese family.
A get together, noise it up, having a good time group.
Yeah, I come from a big family.

I come from a big family.
Numbers not what they it used to be.
Daddy gone, Mother gone. A brother and sister, too.
Still back-slapping, dreaming, clutching each other and
hanging in there. Big family ways never go away!

THE BEGINNING

Cambridge summer in Commonwealth Mass.
A rainy day cold and a library pass.
Pete and Marie, matchmakers pacing the floor.
Left their own apartment and locked the door.
And I remember.

Talking all night, just you and me.
Glasses of wine and cups of tea.
Early rising, feeling cool like in the shade.
A so long embrace, friendship made.
And I remember.

Kisses, each like the first, so sweet.
Whispered secrets, and vows to keep.
Catching movies, trains and butterflies.
Making measured plans with dreams for our lives.
And I remember.

Discussing Fanon, Langston Hughes, and Malcolm X.
Chastising, criticizing, to keep each other in check.
Iron-willed Vera and dear Camille, too.
In Seventy-one and Seventy-two.
And I remember.

Writing poems meant only for your eyes.
Recording them all just to surprise.
Sonnets of love, a love supreme.
Like a sky-high king, serenading his queen.
And I remember.

Singing our songs and taking our stand,
On liberation while holding hands.
Choosing our own common destiny.
Together, we knew, we held the key.
And I remember.

Time goes by as it has in the past.
Leaving children, gray hair and memories that last.
Ah! But the beginning is always at hand.
It helped to build the foundation on which we now stand.
And I remember.

FALLING IN LOVE

What can I say?
What words can I reach for?
Grab?
Should I cry out in joy to the Ultimate?
Breathing heavily in your ear?
Squeezing your hand like the end is now?
Or should I reach inside of me?
Pull out my essence
And give it to you?
Words just don't seem appropriate
For this moment.

FOR KATURA, FOR STEPHAN

My daughter, my son, I love you!
I loved you before you came.
I knew you were coming, you two.
I had even considered your names.

During my youthful days I dreamed of you,
and when I considered your mother-to-be.
As I pressed for a world that was new,
I knew you would be waiting for me.

Katura, you were our first one.
You quickly claimed your place.
Shining brightly like the sun,
and moving at your own pace.

For six years you reigned supreme,
As this trio took flight.
Adding to the family's esteem.
Creating yours in your own right.

Stephan, then it was time for *your* joy.
We had waited patiently.
And when the doctor said you were a boy,
we couldn't contain our glee.

You brought a new dynamic,
an energy too fiery to hold.
Sometimes leaving us in a panic,
as you pushed for your own goals.

What a journey we four have shared!
What milestones we have gained.
What challenges we have dared.
What landmarks still remain.

Your own path you have blazed.
Your legacy you now create,
Building on those youthful days,
reaching for stars that still await.

PERSONAL REFLECTIONS

REMEMBER

Remember that first dance, that party you weren't supposed to attend?
Remember that kiss, that first kiss, that made you suspend,
All reality as the world seemed to bow at your feet?
And your youthful fantasies were all made complete.
      Remember?

Remember that song, your own national anthem you used to sing?
Remember that favorite shirt, those jeans, onto which you would cling,
As you played it cool, trying to look fresh, saluting the newest trend?
Those youthful days of innocence when all was quite simple then.
      Remember?

Those formative years soon surrender to a more forbidding pace.
Of rushing, pushing, sometimes sprinting, in a quite seductive chase.
For goals and honors and accolades, and unreasoned challenges to win.
Ah! But those youthful days of innocence when all was quite simple then!
      Remember?

TOMORROW

Just in case you missed it,
Tomorrow really did come.

And put all the naysayers,
Hastily on the run.

They sought its demise,
Dying in its sleep.

Leaving all of us, with promises
We couldn't keep.

But tomorrow did come.
As it has done before.

Revealing and exposing,
What it had in store.

AGING

Have you ever wondered how time operates?
I'm not trying to be funny, I'm serious.
I was minding my own business. Doing my own thing.
And time just snatched me up and took me with it
To some distant sphere.
And when I opened my eyes,
Gray hair, a paunchy middle and
Aching bones were now my friends.

Someone said time comes like a thief in the night.
Another said it sneaks up on you like a stone-cold criminal.
Well, maybe that's all true.
But I have come to realize that time does
What it's supposed to do.
It keeps on coming.
Like Sterling Brown's Strong Men,
It keeps on coming.

TEARS

Some folks say a man ain't supposed to cry.
I double down — chest up — and ask, Why?
Been through too much to stop the rain.
Tears need to create their modifying refrain.

Seen hunger bear-hug a precious little child.
Seen death come in and linger for a while.
Seen dreams dry up like a raisin in the sun.
Seen many lives gamed, just for fun.

Seen truth twisted, left blowing in the wind.
Seen sunny days darkened and made sunny again.
Seen homes destroyed by billion-dollar games.
Seen violence loosed, unbridled and unrestrained.

Seen school children lose their desire to learn.
Seen churches drop God as they make their run.
Seen brother fighting brother all over the world.
Seen a struggling humanity desperate for love.

Some folks say a man ain't supposed to cry.
I double down — chest up — and ask, Why?
Because after the tears, more clarity comes.
Roll up the sleeves and get the job done.

OPPORTUNITY

I waited for you.
Got myself a cup of sassafras tea,
a soft, sturdy seat to rest on.
Patiently, I waited for you.

I waited for you,
while whistling a song
and another cup of sassafras.
Alarmed, I waited for you.

I waited for you,
Pacing the floor nervously,
with my third cup of tea.
Angry now, but I waited for you.

I waited for you.
But I finally realized you won't come to me.
To embrace your offerings,
I must go to you. I cannot wait!

SMOOTH OPERATOR

Everyone takes notice whenever he's around.
He's a perfect Jim Dandy, a man about town.
He dresses neat
From head to feet
A cooler dude just can't be found.

Some ladies say that he's a real dream
With cars and money and quite proper esteem.
He'll flip you ten
And call you a friend.
But does he know what freedom really means?

LEGACY

When considering the race that I have run
on this side of time's divide.
Don't mention the frivolous things I have done.
But how I have helped others to reach their stride.

What matters are lives that I have touched,
the children I have helped to stand.
But not the accolades and honors too much.
They will blow away with the sand.

A smile, a touch, a kind word or two,
To better someone else's lot.
Are better measures of me, that's true!
Whether others recognize them or not.

When considering the years that were my gift.
When the last note has been proclaimed.
Count my efforts to uplift.
To leave a world that's better that was my aim!

PASS IT ON

Whenever I feel low. Whenever I'm in despair.
I close my eyes and see my ancestors standing there.
Those who withstood the whip, endured the gruesome pain,
of children sold away, never to be seen again.

Whenever I feel low, feeling that the word is against me.
I see my ancestors standing there, no chance to be free.
But never giving up, holding on in every way.
For the future of their descendants who would be free one day.

Whenever I feel low. Whenever I think life's not fair.
I close my eyes and see my ancestors standing there.
"I held on for a reason," they tell me. – *"I endured for a cause!*
Not for you to give up! Not for you to pause!"

So whenever I feel low. Whenever I'm about to pitch it in.
I see my ancestors standing there, imploring me once again.
I now hold the torch to shine a more radiant light.
To help those to come, brighten their darkest night.

THE BLUES GOT ME!

The Blues got me.
Standing on the corner,
In the pouring rain. Vulnerable.
No coat. No hat! Drenched!
The Blues got me!

The Blues got me.
Wasn't bothering anybody. Don't think so.
Just chillin', minding my own business.
Hope and dreams intact.
But the Blues got me.

The Blues got me.
Not the smooth, soft, velvety kind.
No! It was the low down, dirty, gut-wrenching,
Saw-dust-on-the-floor, couple-grinding, whiskey-smelling kind.
The Blues got me.

The Blues got me.
Smacked me upside the head.
Snatched me by the collar, jacked me up against the wall.
Then dared me to do anything about it.
Yeah! The Blues got me.

The Blues got me.
But I'm no willing victim.
I snap and pop! And jump to attention.
Curtis Mayfield said *keep on pushin'*,
if the Blues got you.

The Blues had me.
But it can't feast on determination and a fighting spirit.
No home here.
See, I'm a long-time fighter, a daring survivor.
So, the Blues let me go.

NEW LEGACY

Walking tall, stilted like, feeling so good.
Tall and Black, strong like ebony wood.
Strutting, pulling, reaching, high among the stars,
And other celestial bodies, like Jupiter and Mars.

It's where I ought to be,
Bebopping, cloud hopping, loose and free.
Aesthetically cool in an awesome way.
Loving myself more every day.

Smelling the flowers along the avenue
Feeling the grass and the just fallen dew.
New realities to fill my memory bank.
Hot dropping words like *don't* and *can't*.

Walking tall, stilted like, feeling so good.
Tall and black, strong like ebony wood.
Langston Hughes asked, *Don't you wanna' be free?*
I shout, *"Yes, I do!",* Langston! I'm creating a new legacy!

FEAR - THE LONG JOURNEY

What is the meaning?
This cold dampness wetting
     my feet, my mind,
     seeping through the pores in
     my body.
Reaching my blood stream.
     It is cold!
     It is cold!
     It is so cold!!!
I am trembling/shaking,
     like something jelled,
     like a scared criminal,
     about to commit a crime.
My fingers are numb
     like ice
     ungrippable
     inhuman.
What is the meaning?

What is this madness?
     Gripping me, pulling me
     to its bosom/inside of it
     smothering me
     with chills and coldness
     caressing me with its
     pain-filled arms, loving me
     with its heart of ice.
What is this?

What is the meaning?
     of the stillness in my mind
     these icicle thoughts
     breaking off easily
     that will melt at sunrise
     But, oh, This winter of me!
It is so cold!

DISTANT TRAVELER

To land, to sea, to yonder's claim.
'Til immortal seeking calls my name.
To run to distant yearning's glow.
To places traveler's pine to know.
No familiar land shall cast my feet.
No intimate setting shall I make complete.
Tis the inquirer's race I care to run.
To feel the radiance of a far-flung sun.
Yesterday's story is a bygone plot.
Reach for tomorrow's, whether obtainable or not.
Long distant thinking shall shape my turn.
Unknown vistas to view, many tracks to churn.

WHO IS HE?

He burst through the fog like a fire-breathing dragon,
Splitting verbs and dangling participles,
Shooting words like bullets to kill and destroy.
He was no Morning Glory blooming beautifully at dawn.
Maybe Jimson Weed, long time caustic and harmful.
From where did he come?

He uncovered scars and clawed new ones,
Exposed for all to see and ponder,
And they were nourished to grow and fester,
To overwhelm the body for an old cause determined to linger.
Is he the purveyor? The agent of this regress?
If so, from where did he come?

He dressed his spell in magic, though it wasn't needed at all.
A Svengali was just an excuse
To help explain old desires and ideas too meaningful to let go.
Healing and wholeness are progress, and progress is
An albatross too much for some to bear.
From where did he come? He has always been here!

JOURNEY

There is a road we all must travel.
Often it is a challenging one.
Where it goes is a question to ponder.
When it ends, all is done.

Sometimes the road is lonesome.
At times there is a crowd afield.
Giving what it likes,
Taking what it will.

All roads have their contours,
To figure out and to navigate.
How we manage to travel them,
determines our eventual fate.

Mine has been quite a journey.
I have faced my travel with awe.
I have embraced my unfolding trip.
That has made the difference thus far!

There are causes I have undertaken.
Injustices I have addressed.
Movements I have embraced,
As I reach for more progress.

There are friends that I have made,
many I would not have known,
had I not pursued this road
That leads me ultimately home.

More road yet before me.
More miles still to go.
I travel on determinedly.
My integrity still in tow.